Best Easy Day Hikes Series

Best Easy Day Hikes
Joshua Tree
National Park

Third Edition

Polly and Bill Cunningham
Revised by Bruce Grubbs

FALCON GUIDES

GUILFORD, CONNECTICUT

FALCONGUIDES®

An imprint of The Rowman & Littlefield Publishing Group, Inc.
4501 Forbes Blvd., Ste. 200
Lanham, MD 20706
www.rowman.com

Falcon and FalconGuides are registered trademarks and Make Adventure Your Story is a trademark of The Rowman & Littlefield Publishing Group, Inc.

Distributed by NATIONAL BOOK NETWORK

Copyright © 2010 The Rowman & Littlefield Publishing Group, Inc.
This FalconGuides edition 2019

Maps by The Rowman & Littlefield Publishing Group, Inc.

British Library Cataloguing in Publication Information available

Library of Congress Cataloging-in-Publication Data available

ISBN 978-1-4930-3990-6 (paperback)
ISBN 978-1-4930-3991-3 (e-book)

∞™ The paper used in this publication meets the minimum requirements of American National Standard for Information Sciences—Permanence of Paper for Printed Library Materials, ANSI/ NISO Z39.48-1992.

Printed in the United States of America

The authors and The Rowman & Littlefield Publishing Group, Inc. assume no liability for accidents happening to, or injuries sustained by, readers who engage in the activities described in this book.

To the thousands of citizens of California and elsewhere, past and present, who laid the groundwork for protection of a large portion of the California desert; to those who helped secure passage of the California Desert Protection Act; and to the dedicated park rangers and naturalists charged with the stewardship of California's irreplaceable desert wilderness.

Contents

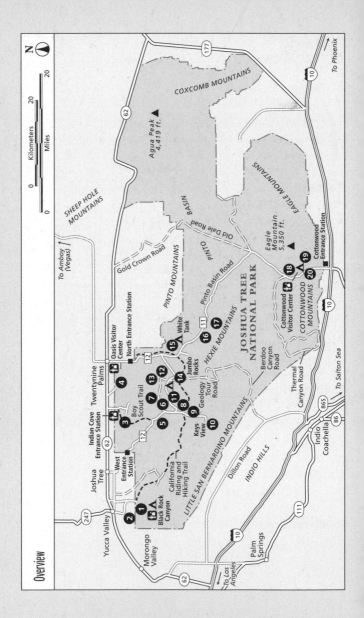

Overview

Introduction

This edition of *Best Easy Day Hikes Joshua Tree National Park* is a shortened and updated version of the Joshua Tree National Park section of *Hiking California's Desert Parks*. This compact guidebook features easily accessible hikes that appeal to the full spectrum of day-hiking visitors—from kids to their grandparents. These twenty hikes sample the best that Joshua Tree National Park has to offer for the casual hiker.

Straddling the transition between the Sonoran (or Colorado) and Mojave Deserts and featuring unique and enchanting granite rock formations, Joshua Tree National Park is a refuge of wild open space close to Los Angeles and next door to the sprawling desert communities of Palm Springs, Joshua Tree, and Yucca Valley.

Joshua Tree was upgraded from national monument to national park status by the 1994 California Desert Protection Act and was enlarged from 559,995 acres to 794,000 acres. The 1994 act also increased wilderness designation to 630,800 acres—70 percent of the park. Mountain ranges define the park's boundaries and dominate its interior. The best-known geologic feature in Joshua Tree is its ethereal landscape of gargantuan monzogranite boulders, domes, and peaks, formed by more than 180 million years of uplifting and erosion.

Hiking in the park quickly reveals contrasts between Sonoran and Mojave Desert vegetation. Below 3,000 feet, the Sonoran Desert encompasses Pinto Basin and other expanses in the southeast portion of the park. This desert is lower, drier, and hotter, supporting creosote bush, ocotillo, sagebrush, and cholla. The higher, moister Mojave Desert, in the northwestern half of the park, is the domain of Joshua tree forests. Forests of pinyon-juniper mixed with manzanita adorn mountain slopes, with smoke trees and mesquite in the washes. Joshua trees, namesake of the park, are shallow rooted and slow growing, taking hundreds of years to reach a mature height of 30 feet. Despite the name, they aren't really trees, however. Joshua "trees" are actually members of the yucca family and lack tree rings.

Five desert oases mark the rare occurrences of both water and concentrated wildlife. Most wildlife is nocturnal and usually invisible to the human eye. Coyotes are common but are only one of 350 vertebrate species that range the park, from ubiquitous mice and wood rats to a desert tortoise that is listed as threatened under the Endangered Species Act. Twenty species of snakes and fourteen kinds of lizards slither and dart across the desert floor, primarily at night. Equally exciting is the array of birds at Joshua Tree, with more than 230 species on the checklist.

Most of the hikes in *Best Easy Day Hikes Joshua Tree National Park* are short—less than 4 miles round-trip and with less than 800 feet of elevation change. More than half the hikes are ideal for families with small children. We have left it up to the parents to determine whether a hike is suitable for their offspring. Child ratings are highly subjective. Two of the hikes, Cap Rock and Keys View, are barrier-free and wheelchair accessible. All the trailheads are reachable by passenger car, and most have a paved road leading to them.

To provide a geographic reference, hikes 1 through 4 are located on the northern edge of the park. They are accessible from the Twentynine Palms Highway (CA 62) in the towns of Yucca Valley, Joshua Tree, and Twentynine Palms. Hikes 5 through 15 are in the heart of the park, within the Mojave Desert ecosystem. The last five hikes are in the southeast region of the park, and thus are located in the Sonoran

Desert. This region of the park is served by the Cottonwood Visitor Center, 8 miles north of I-10, on the southern side of the park.

Note that there is a park entrance fee charged per vehicle, and it is valid for seven days. America the Beautiful, Senior, and Access passes are honored as well.

Before your visit, it is strongly recommended that you contact the park at (760) 367-5500 for current information on fees, park regulations, weather, campgrounds, park resources, and trail conditions. You can also check the park's website at nps.gov/jotr.

Campgrounds

There is a fee at each of the nine campgrounds in the park. To reserve a campsite in one of the more developed campgrounds (Black Rock, Cottonwood, Indian Cove, and Jumbo Rocks), book online at recreation.gov or call (877) 444-6777. The other campgrounds are first-come, first-served. Check the Joshua Tree National Park website (nps.gov/jotr) for the amenities at the various sites.

Website

The park's official website is nps.gov/jotr. You can check the website for weekly ranger programs, including the guided walks that are offered primarily in the spring and fall. The walks are free and require no reservations, with the exception of the 0.5-mile Desert Queen Ranch Tour.

Regulations Pertinent to Day Hiking

Federal law protects all plants and wildlife in the park. No hunting or collecting of any kind is permitted. Gathering firewood or any vegetation is also forbidden in the park. Fires are allowed only in established fire rings within the campgrounds.

Dogs and other pets must remain within 100 yards of roads and campgrounds and must be leashed at all times. Because they are not allowed on trails, they should be left at home.

Respect private land inholdings by closing gates and staying off private land when posted.

Before you begin hiking, be sure to stop at one of the visitor centers or a ranger station to get updated regulations. These rules are designed to protect your safety as well as the ecological integrity of Joshua Tree National Park.

Play It Safe

Wandering in the desert has a reputation of being a dangerous activity, thanks to both the Bible and Hollywood. Usually depicted as a wasteland, the desert evokes fear. With proper planning, however, desert hiking is not hazardous. In fact, it is fun, exciting, and quite safe.

An enjoyable desert outing requires preparation. Begin with this book, along with the maps suggested in the hike descriptions, to equip yourself with adequate knowledge about your hiking area.

Regardless of how short a hike may be, it is always wise to carry water. In the dry desert area, your body loses water insensibly, without sweating, and you can become dehydrated without realizing it. Dehydration, if not prevented, leads to heat exhaustion and eventually to sunstroke—a life-threatening emergency. So carrying water is not enough—take the time to stop and drink it. Frequent water breaks are mandatory. It is best to return from your hike with empty water bottles. Carry backup water in your vehicle so you'll have some when you finish your hike. And to keep your electrolytes in balance, eat plenty of snacks such as nuts and fresh or dried fruit.

Weather

Daytime temperatures from June through September average around 100°F. Comfortable hiking weather is the norm during the rest of the year, although May can get toasty. High and low temperatures of 85°F and 50°F, respectively, typify spring and fall. July and August often bring brief thunderstorms. Winter may bring highs of up to 60°F, along with freezing nights and occasional rain or snow showers. Desert hikers need to be prepared for ever-changing climatic conditions.

The desert is well known for sudden shifts in the weather. The temperature can change 50°F in less than 1 hour, especially during thunderstorms. Prepare yourself with extra food and clothing, including rain and wind gear.

Hypothermia/Hyperthermia

Abrupt chilling is as much a danger in the desert as heat stroke. Storms and/or nightfall can cause desert temperatures to plunge in any season. Wear layers of clothes, adding or subtracting depending on conditions, to avoid overheating or chilling. At the other extreme, you need to protect yourself from sun and wind with proper clothing. The broad-brimmed hat is mandatory equipment for the desert traveler. Even in the cool days of winter, a delightful time in the desert, the sun's rays are intense. Do not forget the sunscreen.

Mine Hazards

Joshua Tree National Park contains hundreds of deserted mines—consider all of them hazardous. When it comes to mines and mine structures, stay out and stay alive. The edges of mine shafts are often unstable and can collapse if you venture too close. Old mines can also contain invisible but dangerous gases such as radon. The vast majority of these mines have not been secured or even posted. Keep an eye on young or adventuresome members of your group.

Flash Floods and Road Closures

Desert washes and canyons can become traps for unwary visitors when rainstorms hit the desert. Keep a watchful eye on the sky. A storm anywhere upstream in a drainage can cause a sudden torrent in a lower canyon. Do not cross a flooded wash by foot or vehicle. Both the depth and the current can be deceiving; wait for the flood to recede, which usually does not take long. Check on regional weather conditions at a ranger station before embarking on your backcountry expedition. The Cottonwood Canyon Road can be impassable due to flooding, and the unpaved road to the Desert Queen Mine and Pine City sites can also be damaged by storms.

Lightning

Be aware of lightning, especially during summer storms. Stay off ridges and peaks. You should also avoid shallow overhangs and gullies, because electrical current often moves at ground level near a lightning strike.

Giardia

Any surface water is apt to contain *Giardia lamblia*, a microorganism that causes severe diarrhea. It is unwise to trust any water you find flowing in the park. Please note: All water sources in the park are now protected.

Zero Impact

The desert environment is fragile: Damage lasts for decades—even centuries. Desert courtesy requires us to leave no evidence that we were ever there. This ethic means no graffiti or defoliation at one end of the spectrum, and no unnecessary footprints on delicate vegetation on the other. The Leave No Trace ethic includes:

- Leave with everything you brought with you.
- Leave no sign of your visit.
- Leave the landscape as you found it.

To leave no trace of your visit, abide by these suggestions:

- Avoid making new trails or exploring private inholdings. If hiking cross-country, stay on one set of footprints when traveling in a group. Try to make your route invisible.

- Leave your pets at home. Joshua Tree regulations forbid dogs on trails, and no one should leave an animal in a vehicle—the desert heat will kill them. Share experiences other than the desert with your best friend.

- Pack it in and pack it out. This is truer in the desert than anywhere else. Desert winds spread debris, and desert air preserves it. Always carry a trash bag, both for your trash and for any that you encounter. If you must smoke, pick up your butts and bag them. Bag and carry out toilet paper (it does not deteriorate in the desert) and feminine hygiene products.

- Treat human waste properly. Bury human waste 4 inches deep and at least 200 feet from water and trails. Do not burn toilet paper; many wildfires have been started this way. Always use toilets when they are present. Fortunately vault toilets are plentiful in the park. Most trailheads have them.

- Respect wildlife. Living in the desert is hard enough without being harassed by human intruders. Be respectful and use binoculars for long-distance viewing. Do not contaminate the rare desert water sources by playing or bathing in them.

- Respect historical artifacts. Federal law and park regulations forbid disturbing or removing historical evidence over fifty years old. Leave the old miners' things right where they left them so that the explorers who follow you can enjoy the thrill of discovery too.

How to Use This Guide

This guide is designed to be simple and easy to use. Each hike is described with a map and summary information that delivers the trail's vital statistics including length, difficulty, trailhead facilities, and trail surface. Directions to the trailhead are also provided, along with a general description of what you'll see along the way. A detailed route finder (Miles and Directions) sets forth mileages between significant landmarks along the trail.

Types of Hikes

This guide describes two types of hikes.

- **Loop:** A loop hike begins and ends at the same trailhead without duplication of all or most of the route. Loop mileage is provided.
- **Out-and-back:** Out-and-back hikes reach a specific destination and return via the same route. Round-trip mileage is provided.

How and When to Get There

CA 62 (Twentynine Palms Highway) travels along the park's northern boundary. The Park Boulevard entrance is south of the town of Joshua Tree. There is a visitor center at the intersection of CA 62 and Park Boulevard. Farther to the east, in Twentynine Palms, the park headquarters and visitor center is south of CA 62 on Utah Trail (which becomes Park Boulevard when it enters the park). The ancient Oasis of Mara is located adjacent to the visitor center. Joshua Tree National Park is bounded on the south by I-10. The Cottonwood entrance to the park's south end is 65 miles west of Blythe and 52 miles east of Palm Springs.

The park is open year-round, but the best times to visit Joshua Tree are during the cooler months of October through April. The annual wildflower bloom begins in the lower Sonoran Desert in February and spreads to the higher Mojave Desert in March and April. The wildflower hotline is (760) 767-4684.

Maps

The map referred to in the map section for each hike is the Joshua Tree National Park Trail map (#226), a topographic backcountry and hiking map at 1:80,000 scale, published by National Geographic as part of their Trails Illustrated series. In general, the more detailed 7.5-minute USGS quad maps (1:24,000 scale) listed for each hike are not needed unless venturing beyond the described route. Other sources for detailed topographic maps include gaiagps.com and caltopo .com. Refer to the small-scale maps in this book, especially for shorter nature trails that are typically well signed.

Ranking the Hikes

The following list ranks the hikes in this book from easiest to most challenging.

10	Keys View (wheelchair accessible)
8	Cap Rock Nature Trail (wheelchair accessible)
17	Cholla Cactus Garden Nature Trail
15	Arch Rock Nature Trail
3	Indian Cove Nature Trail
20	Cottonwood Spring Nature Trail
5	Hidden Valley Nature Trail
7	Wall Street Mill
6	Barker Dam Nature Trail
14	Skull Rock Nature Trail
7	Wonderland Wash
20	Moorten's Mill Site
13	Pine City Site
9	Lost Horse Mine
2	South Park Peak
1	High View Nature Trail
12	Desert Queen Mine and Wash
16	Silver Bell Mine
18	Mastodon Peak
4	Fortynine Palms Oasis
10	Inspiration Peak
11	Ryan Mountain
19	Lost Palms Oasis

Trail Finder

Hikes for Birders

Hikes for Panoramic Views

Historical Hikes

Mining Sites

Nature Trails

Legend

Transportation

═〔10〕═	Interstate Highway
═〔62〕═	State Highway
═〔12〕═	Park/Other Road
= = = =	Unpaved Road

Trails

▬ ▬ ▬ ▬	Featured Trail
- - - - -	Trail
→	Direction of Route

Water Features

⬭	Body of Water
—··—··—	Intermittent Creek
⌐	Spring

Symbols

🔟2	Trailhead
■	Building/Point of Interest
🏢	Park Office
🅿	Parking
🚻	Restroom
📷	Scenic View
?	Visitor Center
⊞	Picnic Area
⛰	Campground
▲	Mountain/Peak
∩	Cave/Arch
○	Towns and Cities

Land Management

▢	National Park

Hikes on the
Northern Edge

1 High View Nature Trail

The High View Trail, as the name suggests, provides panoramic views of the park's western section. The gently graded climb offers plenty of opportunities to pause—some with a nearby bench—to enjoy the vista. An interpretive brochure is available at the Black Rock Ranger Station.

Distance: 1.3-mile loop
Approximate hiking time: 2 hours
Difficulty: Moderate due to a 320-foot elevation gain
Trail surface: Sandy earth with some rocky steps

Maps: Trails Illustrated Joshua Tree National Park map; USGS Yucca Valley South
Trailhead facilities: The parking area is at the end of a short dirt road. A vault toilet is available at the adjacent Black Rock Campground.

Finding the trailhead: From CA 62 in Yucca Valley, turn south on Avalon Avenue and drive 0.7 mile to where it becomes Palomar Avenue. Continue south on Palomar Avenue for 2.3 miles and turn left on Joshua Lane. Take Joshua Lane for 1 mile to a T intersection at San Marino Drive. Turn right and go 0.3 mile to Black Rock Road. Turn left on Black Rock Road and drive south 0.5 mile to the park's entrance. Immediately before the entrance, turn right (west) onto a dirt road and go 0.8 mile to the parking area. GPS: N34 4.579' / W116 23.966'

The Hike

This nature trail travels to the top of a hill, providing a view over the Yucca Valley and the northern reaches of the park. There is a register at the summit at 0.5 mile, as well as a

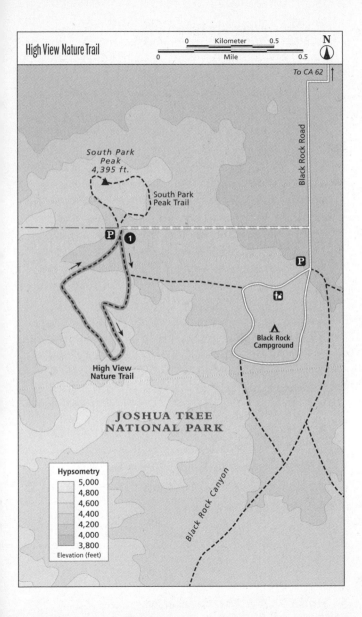

High View Nature Trail

0   Kilometer   0.5

0   Mile   0.5

N

To CA 62

Black Rock Road

South Park
Peak
4,395 ft.

South Park
Peak Trail

P ❶

P

Black Rock
Campground

High View
Nature Trail

JOSHUA TREE
NATIONAL PARK

Black Rock Canyon

Hypsometry

| 5,000 |
| 4,800 |
| 4,600 |
| 4,400 |
| 4,200 |
| 4,000 |
| 3,800 |

Elevation (feet)

bench. The 1.3-mile-long trail follows a relatively gentle route as it climbs 320 feet. Numbered sites line the trail; brochures are available at the Black Rock Ranger Station in the adjacent campground. Even without a brochure in hand this is a delightful overview of Joshua Tree, both the town and the park.

From the parking area, go directly south to begin the hike. The climb to the peak is moderated by the winding pathway. The descent leads down the back side of the peak, then curves around to the north to return to the parking lot. For those with tender knees, the longer descent allows for a gentler grade and is easier on your joints than a shorter route down. Also, the back side of the peak gives you a real flavor of desert solitude. No automobiles, no roads, no bustle, no noise.

If you're staying at the nearby Black Rock Campground, a hilly but very scenic route connects the campground with the nature trail. It leaves from the top of the campground loop above the ranger station and enters the nature loop in its first section. Although clearly marked, this alternate route to the campground has an aura of wilderness. On our loop hike from the campground, we spotted two coyotes hunting for rabbits in the middle of the afternoon. This extension to the peak hike adds 1 mile to the total distance.

Miles and Directions

0.0 Start by heading directly south from the parking area.

0.5 Reach the summit; go straight ahead to continue the loop.

1.3 Arrive back at the trailhead.

2 South Park Peak

From the summit you will enjoy sweeping vistas of the northwestern section of the park as well as the sea of towns beyond the park boundaries. The value of protecting land through park designation is nicely illustrated by this juxtaposition of uses.

Distance: 0.7-mile loop
Approximate hiking time: 1 hour
Difficulty: Moderate due to a 250-foot elevation gain
Trail surface: Sandy earth with some rock steps

Maps: Trails Illustrated Joshua Tree National Park map; USGS Yucca Valley South
Trailhead facilities: The parking area is at the end of a dirt road. A vault toilet is in the nearby Black Rock Campground.

Finding the trailhead: From CA 62 in Yucca Valley, take Avalon Avenue south for 0.7 mile to where it becomes Palomar Avenue. Continue south on Palomar Avenue for 2.3 miles to Joshua Lane. Turn left onto Joshua Lane and drive 1 mile to the T intersection with San Marino Drive. Turn right on San Marino Drive and go 0.3 mile to its end at Black Rock Road. Turn left (south) on Black Rock Road and go 0.5 mile to the park entrance. Immediately before the entrance, turn right (west) on the dirt road. Follow it for 0.8 mile to the parking area. The unsigned trail to the peak begins at the northwest corner of the parking area. GPS: N34 4.579' / W116 23.966'

The Hike

Although this short loop hike lies just outside Joshua Tree National Park's northern boundary, it provides a sweeping

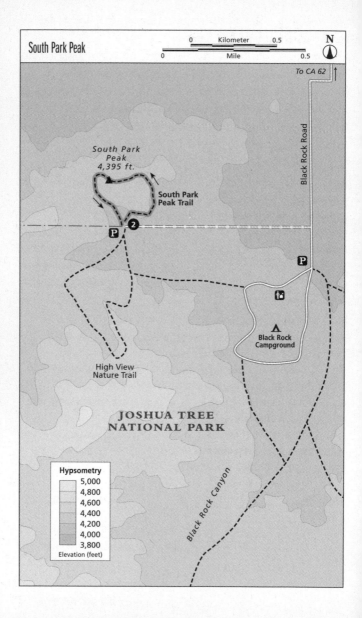

South Park Peak

0 Kilometer 0.5

0 Mile 0.5

N

To CA 62

Black Rock Road

South Park Peak 4,395 ft.

South Park Peak Trail

P

2

P

Black Rock Campground

High View Nature Trail

JOSHUA TREE NATIONAL PARK

Black Rock Canyon

Hypsometry

5,000
4,800
4,600
4,400
4,200
4,000
3,800

Elevation (feet)

view of the park's northwestern section and the town of Joshua Tree in the valley below.

Take the right-hand trail north of the parking area. This gentle peak climb begins as an easy dirt trail. At 0.2 mile there is a comfortable bench where you can enjoy the excellent view. Another bench adorns the summit at 0.4 mile. The trail between the benches is steeper and rockier than the section from the parking area. Pausing to enjoy the view is always an option.

The peak boasts quite a register. With a concrete pedestal and a Plexiglas box, it is an impressive item. The stack of registers within the box makes great reading while you are resting on the bench. Lots of literary visitors climb South Park Peak.

Yucca Valley's sprawl, with its subdivisions closing in on the park, swirls on the north—while to the south lies the vast open space of Joshua Tree National Park. As many that signed the register noted, this sight is confirmation that national park status is the best protection for desert areas, particularly near expanding population centers.

Follow the trail past the register box for your return. The trail descends to the wash on the back side of the peak and ends at the parking area.

Miles and Directions

- **0.0** Start by going north, bearing to your right.
- **0.2** Reach a park bench.
- **0.4** Arrive on the summit of South Park Peak; continue on the loop trail past the register box.
- **0.7** Arrive back at the trailhead.

3 Indian Cove Nature Trail

This nature trail follows a broad desert wash on the northern edge of the Wonderland of Rocks area of the park. The interpretive signs emphasize desert vegetation found in such drainages.

Distance: 0.6-mile loop
Approximate hiking time: Less than 1 hour
Difficulty: Easy
Trail surface: Sandy wash with some scattered rocks

Maps: Trails Illustrated Joshua Tree National Park map; USGS Indian Cove
Trailhead facilities: The parking area is at the western edge of the Indian Cove Campground. There are vault toilets at the campground.

Finding the trailhead: Go 9.8 miles east of Park Boulevard in Joshua Tree on CA 62, then take Indian Cove Road south for 3 miles to Indian Cove Campground. Bear right at the Y intersection and follow the signs for the nature trail parking area. From the east, take CA 62 for 7 miles west of the Utah Trail/CA 62 intersection in Twentynine Palms; take Indian Cove Road south for 3 miles to the campground and follow signs to the parking lot for the nature trail. GPS: N34 5.681' / W116 10.111'

The Hike

This interpretive nature trail is one of the more difficult ones to follow due to the scarcity of arrows, trail indicators, and informational signs. The trail skirts alongside the vast field of boulders that marks the north end of Wonderland of Rocks. The trail begins just west of the parking area, travels across

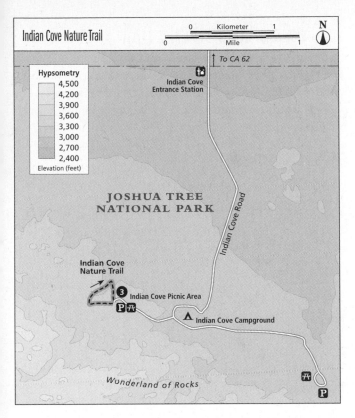

Indian Cove Nature Trail

0 ——— Kilometer ——— 1

0 ——— Mile ——— 1

N

Hypsometry

	4,500
	4,200
	3,900
	3,600
	3,300
	3,000
	2,700
	2,400

Elevation (feet)

↑ To CA 62

Indian Cove
Entrance Station

JOSHUA TREE
NATIONAL PARK

Indian Cove Road

Indian Cove
Nature Trail

3 Indian Cove Picnic Area

P

Indian Cove Campground

Wonderland of Rocks

P

an alluvial fan, and goes down into a broad wash where you bear to your right. A short 0.2 mile later, it exits the wash and returns to the parking area.

The information provided ranges from background on Paleo-Indians to desert plant and animal identification to physical geology. There is no thematic common denominator. The variety of life in a shallow wash is extraordinary.

Like so many desert wash trails, this one is periodically swept by torrents. As a result the trail is periodically erased from the sandy ground. The identification signs are a help in maintaining your pathway on the loop trip.

It is easy to miss the path's exit from the wash. Watch for the identification sign for the desert senna on your right immediately after the paperbag bush sign. That is your signal to bear right out of the wash to pick up the trail back to the parking area.

Miles and Directions

0.0 Follow signs to go west from the parking area.

0.1 Slope down into a wash, following the trail to the right (north).

0.2 Exit the wash, turning to your right.

0.6 Arrive back at the parking area.

4 Fortynine Palms Oasis

Close to the bustle of the town of Joshua Tree, this oasis is a peaceful island of quiet and solitude. Towering California fan palms, perhaps even more than forty-nine of them, are nestled in this canyon oasis.

Distance: 3.0 miles out and back
Approximate hiking time: 3 hours
Difficulty: More strenuous due to distance and a 360-foot eleva-tion gain/loss
Trail surface: Sandy earth with rocky sections
Maps: Trails Illustrated Joshua Tree National Park map; USGS Queen Mountain

Trailhead facilities: This signed end-of-road trailhead has restrooms.
Other: The park service leads a hike on the oasis trail as part of its informative series of programs. Check the park website, or at a ranger station, for the schedule. There is no fee for the program, and reservations are not required.

Finding the trailhead: From CA 62, 11.2 miles east of Park Bou-levard in Joshua Tree, take Fortynine Palms Canyon Road south for 2 miles to its end. From Twentynine Palms, travel 5.5 miles west on CA 62 to the Fortynine Palms Canyon Road exit, then go south for 2 miles to the road's end at the parking area. GPS: N34 7.173' / W116 6.730'

The Hike

This is a clear but rocky trail to the Fortynine Palms Oasis. From the parking lot the trail climbs to its highest point in the first half of the trip. From this elevation you have a view of the town of Twentynine Palms to the north.

Shortly after this high point, at 0.5 mile, the trail jogs sharply to the right. You have your first glimpse of the tall palms, down in a rocky gorge 0.75 mile ahead. The blast of greenery might seem a stereotypical desert mirage, but it will encourage you to proceed. The descent to the oasis traverses dry, rocky terrain; even the desert shrubs are dwarfed by the harsh conditions. Miniature barrel cacti dot the slopes. The windy, dry hills above make the oasis even more striking.

At Fortynine Palms Oasis (1.5 miles), the huge old palms tower above a dense willow thicket that provides a congenial habitat for numerous desert birds. Hummingbirds are frequent visitors. The canyon is also a mecca for desert bighorn sheep. The lushness of the oasis is all the more appealing given the starkness of its surroundings.

In this idyllic setting, the palm trees have a bizarre appearance. Fires have scarred the trunks of these elegant trees. Their lives were spared, and the fronds are untouched. The fires that blacken the trunks, whether caused by lightning or careless humans, may actually benefit the fire--resistant palm trees by clearing out competing vegetation, such as mesquite and arrowweed.

Humans have left their marks also. Knife-wielding visitors have tattooed the trunks with initials, signs, and names. The sight of these assaults on the palms is incongruous in such an idyllic setting. One hopes that more recent visitors have greater respect for these hardy giants and do not assault the trees.

After enjoying some quiet time at the oasis, return to the trailhead by the same route.

Miles and Directions

0.0 The trail begins by going south from the parking area.

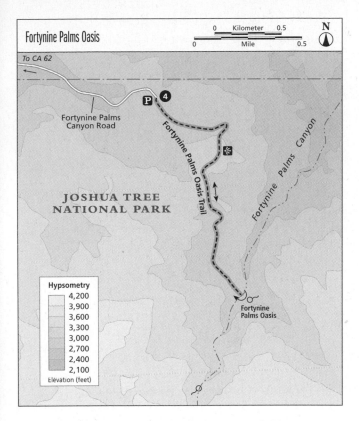

Fortynine Palms Oasis

JOSHUA TREE
NATIONAL PARK

Fortynine Palms
Canyon Road

Fortynine Palms Oasis Trail

Fortynine Palms Canyon

To CA 62

Fortynine
Palms Oasis

Hypsometry

| 4,200 |
| 3,900 |
| 3,600 |
| 3,300 |
| 3,000 |
| 2,700 |
| 2,400 |
| 2,100 |

Elevation (feet)

0.3 The trail turns sharply to the right; continue climbing.

0.5 Climb to the top of the ridge; achieve the first view of the oasis.

1.0 Cross the wash; continue downhill.

1.5 Reach the oasis. Retrace your path to the trailhead.

3.0 Arrive back at the trailhead.

Heart of the Park

5 Hidden Valley Nature Trail

For good reason this is one of the park's most heavily visited trails. The enchanting valley is surrounded by mounds of monzogranite and attracts climbers as well as more casual explorers. The interpretive signs explain the history of the area, geology, and plant life.

Distance: 1.0-mile loop
Approximate hiking time: Less than 1 hour
Difficulty: Easy
Trail surface: Sandy earth
Maps: Trails Illustrated Joshua Tree National Park map; USGS Indian Cove

Trailhead facilities: There is parking and a picnic area with a vault toilet at the trailhead.
Other: The park service features a free ranger program in Hidden Valley. The schedule changes with the seasons, so check the calendar at a ranger station or on the park website. No reservations are required.

Finding the trailhead: From CA 62 in Joshua Tree, take the Park Boulevard exit and head south for 1 mile on Park Boulevard to where it becomes Quail Springs Road. Continue on Quail Springs Road for 4.3 miles to the park's west entrance; stay on the same road (now Park Boulevard/PR 12) for 8.7 miles to Hidden Valley Nature Trail and Picnic Area, which is on your right (south). After you turn off the main road, follow the paved road to the right for less than 0.1 mile to the parking area. GPS: N34 0.724' / W116 10.083'

The Hike

This interpretive trail emphasizes the area's historical uses as it travels the 1–mile perimeter of Hidden Valley with very little change in elevation. The setting is a snug valley surrounded by massive granite formations.

The trail from the parking area winds upward through the boulders to the hidden valley. This part of the trail consists of old asphalt, so following it is easy. The rest of the journey is unpaved, but is clearly marked with signs, arrows, or fallen logs. A bit of the entry trail requires negotiating around and over moderate boulders, but a nice wooden bridge takes you over the most challenging part.

There are occasional pathways diverging in all directions within the level valley (though this hike is essentially a single loop). Most are used by the numerous rock climbers who are attracted to the massive blocks of granite that create the valley walls. It is likely you will hear climbers' shouts echoing off the rocks and spot these adventuresome park visitors dangling on ropes or standing on top of the immense boulders.

To follow the historical signs in chronological order, go left when you enter the valley, 0.1 mile from the trailhead.

Indian life and settlers' activities are the emphasis on the early part of the trail. The abnormally high rainfall (10 inches per year) of the late nineteenth century led to the development of cattle ranching. The McHaney Gang allegedly used Hidden Valley as a base camp for their large rustling operation in the Southwest, until they turned their energies to gold mining. They began developing the Desert Queen Mine in 1895. It was eventually taken over by Bill Keys, who became quite the desert magnate—a successful rancher and miner—before his death in 1969.

The advent of the automobile in the 1920s brought many new visitors to the desert, endangering the fragile environment. In the 1930s, Minerva Hamilton Hoyt led efforts to

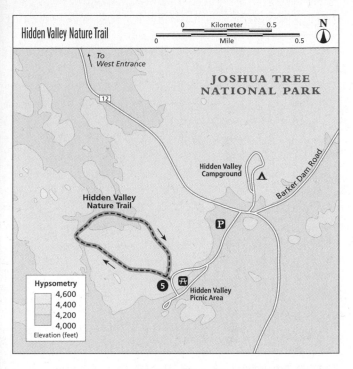

To
West Entrance

Hidden Valley
Campground

Barker Dam Road

Hidden Valley
Nature Trail

P

5

Hidden Valley
Picnic Area

Hypsometry

4,600
4,400
4,200
4,000
Elevation (feet)

protect the region, resulting finally in Franklin D. Roosevelt's 1936 establishment of Joshua Tree National Monument. In 1950, the monument's size was reduced to permit extensive mining. The larger area was restored with the California Desert Protection Act of 1994, when the area was designated a national park. The nature trail provides an overview of this history, as well as a reminder to the visitor to remain vigilant as a protector of desert resources.

Miles and Directions

0.0 From the parking area, the trail goes into the narrow canyon leading to the valley.

0.1 At the junction, follow the trail left around the valley.

0.9 Reach the end of the loop at the original junction. Turn left to return to the parking lot.

1.0 Arrive back at the trailhead.

6 Barker Dam Nature Trail

This popular nature trail leads to the park's only lake, which was created by a rancher's dam. Winter rains often fill the lake, providing habitat for migratory birds—even ducks. This trail is closed to visitors from 6 p.m. to 8 a.m. so desert bighorn sheep can have access to water without human disturbance.

Distance: 1.4-mile loop
Approximate hiking time: 1 hour
Difficulty: Easy
Trail surface: Sandy earth with a few rocky steps along the lake
Maps: Trails Illustrated Joshua Tree National Park map; USGS Indian Cove
Trailhead facilities: There is a signed parking lot and a vault toilet at the trailhead.

Other: The park service leads an informative guided hike at the Barker Dam Trail. There is no fee, and no registration is required. Check the park website or at a ranger station for the schedule, which changes seasonally. Hiking tours meet at the parking area.

Finding the trailhead: From CA 62 in Joshua Tree, take Park Boulevard south for 1 mile to where it becomes Quail Springs Road. Continue on Quail Springs Road for 4.3 miles to the park's west entrance. Follow Park Boulevard (PR 12) for 8.7 miles to a left (east) turn at the Hidden Valley Campground toward Barker Dam. Go straight, past the campground entrance, for 1.6 miles to the Barker Dam parking lot. GPS: N34 1.363' / W116 9.394'

The Hike

This hike provides easy access to the only lake in the park. Since it is located on the edge of the Wonderland of Rocks, the trail is bordered by a jumbled maze of granite boulders interspersed with Joshua trees.

The highly informative Barker Dam Nature Trail is a step back in time, both in terms of prehistory and with respect to futile, short-lived attempts to raise cattle back in the early 1900s. Barker Dam was built by ranchers Barker and Shay in a natural rock catch basin to store water for cattle. In 1949 and 1950, the dam was raised by Bill Keys, owner of the Desert Queen Mine and the nearby Desert Queen Ranch, still a private inholding. When filled to capacity by winter rains, the lake behind the dam encompasses 20 acres. Because it is surrounded by a magnificent rock ring of monzonite granite, it looks almost as though it is nestled in a high Sierra cirque at 11,000 feet. Today, the lake is used by bighorn sheep and many other species of wildlife, including shorebirds and migratory waterfowl—some of the last creatures you would expect to find in the desert!

The trail is clear and sandy, winding through a couple of tight places in the rocks, reaching Barker Dam at 0.5 mile. Notable plant species seen en route include turbinella oak, adapted to the high Mojave Desert above 4,000 feet, and nolina—a yucca look-alike that provided food for the Cahuilla Indians, who used it in baking like molasses.

Below the dam are interesting man-made stone structures. Here, the innovative Bill Keys built stone watering basins designed to prevent spillage of the precious desert water. It could be said that water is more precious than gold here; clever Keys was involved with both commodities.

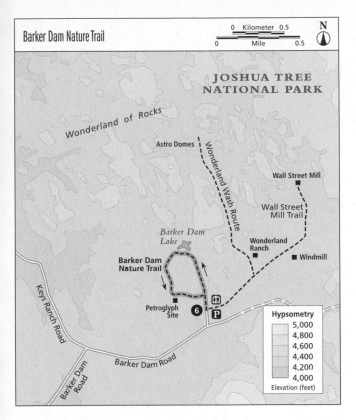

From Barker Dam Lake, the trail heads west and south through a series of intimate little alcove–like valleys containing rock-lined gardens of Joshua trees, cholla cacti, and yucca. Vegetation is being reestablished around this area, so please be careful to avoid trampling the new plantings and other vegetation.

The loop continues back to the junction and then to the parking area.

Miles and Directions

0.0 The trail leaves the parking area going north.

0.2 Bear right at the junction.

0.5 Arrive at Barker Dam Lake.

0.6 Pass a watering trough.

1.0 Reach the petroglyphs.

1.2 Arrive back at the junction; turn right to return to the parking area.

1.4 Arrive at the end of the hike at the parking lot.

7 Wall Street Mill/Wonderland Wash

This well-marked trail takes you to a historic ore processing mill and other remnants of early mining days. The desert climate has remarkable powers of preservation. An easy side trip into the impressive Wonderland of Rocks is available from the Wall Street Mill route.

Distance: 1.5 miles out and back, plus a side trip of approximately 1 mile
Approximate hiking time: 1.5 hours to mill and back; 2 hours with the side trip
Difficulty: Easy

Trail surface: Sandy earth and sandy wash
Maps: Trails Illustrated Joshua Tree National Park map; USGS Indian Cove
Trailhead facilities: There is a paved parking area and a vault toilet.

Finding the trailhead: From CA 62 in Joshua Tree, take Park Boulevard south and drive 1 mile to where it becomes Quail Springs Road. Continue on Quail Springs Road for 4.3 miles to the park's west entrance, where it becomes Park Boulevard (PR 12). Follow the park road southeast for 8.7 miles to Hidden Valley Campground/Barker Dam Road. Turn left (east) at the campground sign. Go past the campground turnoff. Stay on the paved road, past Keys Ranch Road on your left, for 1.6 miles to the Barker Dam parking area. GPS: N34 1.363' / W116 9.394'

The Hike

This level hike displays the desert's power of preservation! Rusty old trucks still have their tires. Antique cars sit peacefully beneath oak trees. The mill, protected on the National

Register of Historic Places due to its local technological and mechanical uniqueness, still stands with its machinery intact, albeit a tad rusty. A barbed wire fence protects the mill from visitors. Nearby are hulks of vehicles and other artifacts of life in the desert from seventy years ago. A park sign at the mill explains its workings and includes an excellent drawing—actually a blueprint of its original design in the 1930s. This is a fun voyage of discovery, even for those who might not be machinery or mining buffs.

From the Barker Dam parking area, take the trail to the right, heading east-northeast. The vast granite Wonderland of Rocks is on your left, and your trail skirts along its edge. At 0.25 mile the trail arrives at the original sandy parking area with an adjacent vault toilet. Continue on the trail to the left of the toilet.

An old windmill stands to the right of the trail at 0.35 mile. Over your shoulder to the left you may spy ranch house ruins. Oddly, they were painted pink. These are remnants of the ranching era in the Queen Valley. The Keys family has been involved in both ranching and mining and still has a private inholding, the Desert Queen Ranch, to the west of this trail.

The Wall Street Mill was part of the Keys industrial complex. Built by Bill Keys to process the ore from the Desert Queen Mine, it was in operation for only a few years before falling into disuse. One reason for its short life span is that Bill Keys had a run-in with Worth Bagley, his neighbor, over the use of the road to the mill. Convicted of murder, Keys spent five years in San Quentin prison but was later exonerated. Apparently he had shot Bagley in self-defense.

Continue on the well-used trail, bending to the north. The Wall Street Mill is at 0.75 mile. You will want to wander around the site, discovering artifacts of the mining era hidden in the shrubbery. Return to the parking area by the same wash/trail.

Option: On your way back to the trailhead, after you pass the windmill, you can more clearly see the remains of Wonderland Ranch off to your right. Head for the house. Follow the beaten path to the left of the house into the nearby shallow wash, only about 50 feet from the house site. The narrow wash is easy to follow, with periodic pathways weaving from bank to bank as you follow it northward into the Wonderland. A plethora of use trails created by hundreds of rock climbing enthusiasts wander into the widening valley of domes.

Plentiful oak and prickly pear, as well as the remnants of a dam in the wash, are other attractions of this hike—but the primary foci are the huge rock formations stretching in all directions in an enchanted world of whimsically eroded granite mounds. Well into the wash (1 mile from the old trailhead) are the formations known to rock climbers who enjoy scaling their massive surfaces as the Astro Domes. You can usually hear climbers' voices echoing from various points among the boulders, and their silhouettes may startle you when they appear hundreds of feet above, atop these obelisks.

The return trip down the wash to the trailhead is equally interesting, providing views of the rock formations from a different perspective. The proximity of the mill and the mounds of monzogranite provide an appropriate contrast between the reign of humans and of nature in this wild country.

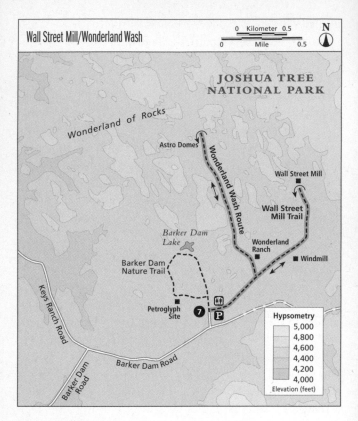

JOSHUA TREE
NATIONAL PARK

Wonderland of Rocks

Astro Domes

Wonderland Wash Route

Wall Street Mill

Wall Street
Mill Trail

Barker Dam
Lake

Wonderland
Ranch

Barker Dam
Nature Trail

Windmill

Petroglyph
Site

Keys Ranch Road

Barker Dam Road

Barker Dam Road

Hypsometry

	Elevation (feet)
	5,000
	4,800
	4,600
	4,400
	4,200
	4,000

Miles and Directions

0.0 From the parking area, take the trail to the right.

0.2 Follow the arrow to the left, out of the wash.

0.25 Arrive at the old trailhead, with a vault toilet. Continue on the marked trail.

0.35 An old windmill appears on your right.

0.75 A park sign reading "Preserve America's Past" appears among the oak trees; the mill site and various vehicles are on your left. Explore the area, then return by the same route.

1.5 Arrive back at the trailhead.

Option:

1.2 After passing the windmill, bear right on the side trail leading toward the ranch house ruins. Continue past the site on a well-traveled path into Wonderland of Rocks.

2.2 After your exploration, turn around and retrace your steps to the main trail.

3.2 Bear right on the main trail, returning toward the trailhead.

3.5 Arrive back at the trailhead.

8 Cap Rock Nature Trail

This short nature trail features interesting monzogranite rock formations, which attract rock climbers as well as casual strollers. The trail is paved and barrier-free.

Distance: 0.4-mile loop
Approximate hiking time: 30 minutes
Difficulty: Easy and wheelchair accessible
Trail surface: Paved and barrier-free

Maps: Trails Illustrated Joshua Tree National Park map; USGS Keys View
Trailhead facilities: Both the parking area and trail are signed and paved.

Finding the trailhead: From CA 62 in Joshua Tree, take Park Boulevard south for 1 mile to where it becomes Quail Springs Road, and continue for 4.3 miles to the park's west entrance. Continue on Park Boulevard (PR 12) for 14 miles to a right turn on Keys View Road. The parking area for the Cap Rock Nature Trail is on the left (east) side of the road, 0.1 mile from the intersection. GPS: N33 59.348' / W116 9.827'

The Hike

This level nature trail is paved and wheelchair accessible, although it has weathered considerably since it was built in 1982. The numerous signs have also weathered; some are almost illegible. The focus of the information is on the desert plants that grow around these fascinating quartz monzogranite boulder piles.

Cap Rock is nearly at the hub of the loop. The huge boulder has a sporty visor-shaped wedge resembling the bill

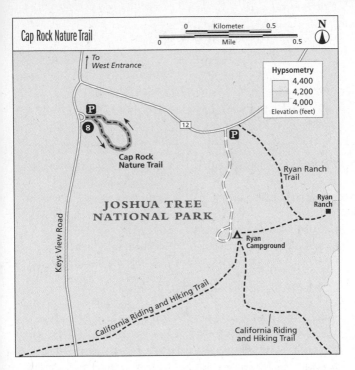

Kilometer
Mile
Hypsometry
4,400
4,200
4,000
Elevation (feet)

↑ To
West Entrance

P
8

Cap Rock
Nature Trail

12

P

Ryan Ranch
Trail

Ryan
Ranch

JOSHUA TREE
NATIONAL PARK

Keys View Road

Ryan
Campground

California Riding and Hiking Trail

California Riding
and Hiking Trail

on a baseball cap. Frequent use by rock climbers makes the 0.4-mile-long Cap Rock Trail an interesting scene, with the silhouettes of climbers like dots against the sky.

Miles and Directions

0.0 From the parking area, start the trail to the right.

0.4 Complete the loop.

⑨ Lost Horse Mine

The hike to this large historic mine site also provides superb views of the Wonderland of Rocks, Malapai Hill, and the vast expanse of Pleasant Valley. The mine is one of the best preserved in Joshua Tree.

Distance: 4.0 miles out and back
Approximate hiking time: 3.5 hours
Difficulty: Moderately strenuous due to distance and a 480-foot elevation gain/loss

Trail surface: Sandy earth with some rocky stretches
Maps: Trails Illustrated Joshua Tree National Park map; USGS Keys View
Trailhead facilities: The parking area is at the end of the unpaved Lost Horse Mine Road.

Finding the trailhead: From CA 62 in the town of Joshua Tree, take Park Boulevard south for 1 mile to where it becomes Quail Springs Road; continue for 4.3 miles to the park's west entrance. Follow Park Boulevard (PR 12) for 14 miles and turn right (south) on Keys View Road (PR 13). Keys View Road is 20 miles southwest of the Oasis Visitor Center at Twentynine Palms by way of Park Boulevard (PR 12). Continue south on Keys View Road for 2.6 miles to the signed Lost Horse Mine Road. Turn left (southeast) and drive to the Lost Horse Mine trailhead, which is at the end of this 1.1-mile-long dirt road. GPS: N33 57.050' / W116 9.593'

The Hike

This multifaceted hike offers a pleasant out-and-back journey to a large mining complex, with an optional side trip to a high panoramic point above the mine.

The clear, wide, but somewhat rocky trail was once a wagon road. It climbs moderately, gaining 300 feet after 1 mile across high desert swales of juniper, yucca, a few stunted Joshua trees, and nolina (commonly called bear grass), a member of the agave family often mistaken for yucca because of its long spear-like leaves.

At 2 miles the doubletrack trail reaches the lower end of Lost Horse Mine. This is the largest essentially intact historic mining site in the park, and you could easily spend several hours studying rock buildings. The largest mine shaft, some 500 feet deep, is covered. However, other smaller ones remain unsecured on the hillsides, so you should be extremely cautious when wandering around this site. The pinyon pines and Joshua trees that once adorned the area were removed to fuel the mine and have yet to grow back.

This was one of the most profitable mines in the park. A German miner named Frank Diebold made the first strike. He was later bought out by prospector Johnny Lang, who happened onto the strike in 1893 while searching for a lost horse. He and his partners began developing the mine two years later. They processed several thousand ounces of gold during the following decade. Their process involved crushing the ore at the mill and then mixing it with "quicksilver" (mercury), which bonded with the gold so that it could be separated from the ore rock. Lang was later forced to sell his share of the mine to Jep Ryan. The end came in 1924 when the elderly Lang died of starvation while walking out from his remote cabin.

After visiting the mine, double back the way you came for an enjoyable round-trip.

Option: For a bird's-eye view of the mine and its surroundings, hike north 0.2 mile on the doubletrack that climbs

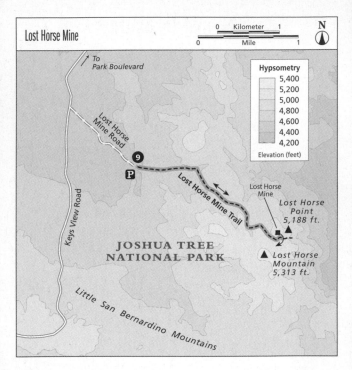

above the fenced-off stamp mill. A short use trail continues up
to Lost Horse Point (5,188 feet), which affords a magnificent
panorama of surrounding basins and peaks, including the Wonderland of Rocks to the north (there is a full 6.5 mile loop
nearby for hikers interested in a more strenuous excursion).

Miles and Directions

0.0 Begin at the Lost Horse Mine trailhead. Follow the old wagon
road toward the mine.

2.0 Reach Lost Horse Mine. Retrace your steps to the trailhead.

4.0 Arrive back at the trailhead.

10 Keys View and Inspiration Peak

Keys View offers spectacular views of the south-central area of the park. An interpretive sign provides information on the serious problem of air pollution in Joshua Tree. To the north of the paved Keys View trail is the route to Inspiration Peak, for more hardy hikers.

Distance: 0.25-mile loop; 1.5 miles out and back for the Inspiration Peak hike
Approximate hiking time: 30 minutes for the loop; 1 hour for the peak
Difficulty: Easy for loop; moderately strenuous for the 525-foot climb to the peak

Trail surface: Paved loop; earthen path to the peak
Maps: Trails Illustrated Joshua Tree National Park map; USGS Keys View
Trailhead facilities: A paved parking area, informational signs, and restrooms are at the trailhead.

Finding the trailhead: From CA 62 in the town of Joshua Tree, take Park Boulevard south for 1 mile to where it becomes Quail Springs Road; continue for 4.3 miles to the park's west entrance. Follow Park Boulevard (PR 12) for 14 miles, then turn right (south) on Keys View Road. Go 5.8 miles to the end of the road and the trailhead. GPS: N33 55.622' / W116 11.252'

The Hike

The clear, paved, barrier-free Keys View path is the highest trail in the park accessible by a paved road. You can count on a brisk breeze, so bring your windbreaker.

The viewpoint is on the crest of the Little San Bernardino Mountains and provides an expansive view of the

Coachella Valley and the San Bernardino Range to the west. Unfortunately, pollution from the Los Angeles basin often obscures the view. Information boards contrasting smog levels give the viewer a good idea of how air pollution affects visibility at differing distances. The smog also endangers the biological integrity of the park itself.

At the lookout there is no diagrammatic map of the park or explanation of the area's geology, a situation often creating questions among visitors to Keys View. Either schedule this trip for late in your stay at Joshua Tree so you will be familiar with the park's landmarks, or bring your park map with you.

A short side trip to Inspiration Peak makes an enjoyable addition for those who like to hike higher. The somewhat steep, rocky trail is well worn and in good condition. Nearly 400 feet are gained to a false summit in the first 0.4 mile.

Look carefully for the trail continuing to the right. It drops 100 feet into a saddle at 0.5 mile and then climbs around the left side, gaining 120 feet in the next 0.25 mile. Keys View sits far below to the south, as do the Coachella Valley and the prominent peaks of the higher San Bernardino Range. The added perspective of the steep canyons and high ridges makes this steep, short climb more than worthwhile. An easily followed use trail continues another 0.1 mile northwest along the main crest until it reaches a mound of large boulders. From Inspiration Peak at 0.75 mile, double back on the same trail, dropping back down to the Keys View parking area.

Miles and Directions

Loop

0.0 The trailhead is at the north end of the Keys View parking area.

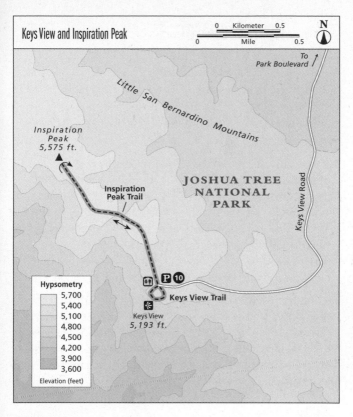

0   Kilometer   0.5

0   Mile   0.5

N

Little San Bernardino Mountains

To
Park Boulevard

Inspiration
Peak
5,575 ft.

Inspiration
Peak Trail

JOSHUA TREE
NATIONAL
PARK

Keys View Road

P **10**

Keys View Trail

Keys View
5,193 ft.

Hypsometry

5,700
5,400
5,100
4,800
4,500
4,200
3,900
3,600

Elevation (feet)

0.25 The loop hike follows the paved path back to the parking lot.

Peak Hike

0.0 Begin the peak hike at the trailhead marked with a hiker symbol.

0.4 Ascend to the first (false) summit (5,558 feet).

0.5 Reach the saddle (5,460 feet).

0.75 Approach the summit of Inspiration Peak (5,575 feet). Retrace your steps toward the trailhead.

1.5 Arrive back at the trailhead.

11 Ryan Mountain

A hike up Ryan Mountain provides a spectacular panorama from the center of the park. The route is steep in places, with rocky steps, but the reward in achieving the summit is worth the effort.

Distance: 3.0 miles out and back
Approximate hiking time: 3 hours
Difficulty: Moderately strenuous due to a 1,070-foot elevation gain/loss and rocky trail surface
Trail surface: Earth, rocks, and rock steps

Maps: Trails Illustrated Joshua Tree National Park map; USGS Indian Cove and Keys View
Trailhead facilities: There is a paved parking area at the signed trailhead.

Finding the trailhead: From CA 62 in Joshua Tree, drive south on Park Boulevard for 1 mile to where it becomes Quail Springs Road. Continue 4.3 miles to the park's west entrance. Follow Park Boulevard (PR 12) for 12.5 miles to the Ryan Mountain trailhead on your right (south). The signed parking area is 2.1 miles east of the junction with Keys View Road. GPS: N34 0.156' / W116 8.165'

The Hike

The trail leaves the parking area through a massive boulder gate of White Tank granite sculpted by selective erosion. This well-signed official park trail is quite a display of rock workmanship. Steeper portions of the trail, beginning at 0.4 mile, feature stair steps artfully constructed from the plentiful native rocks, so it is easy walking up, and there is no skidding going down. The slopes of Ryan Mountain are dotted with ancient metamorphic rocks of schist and gneiss, perhaps

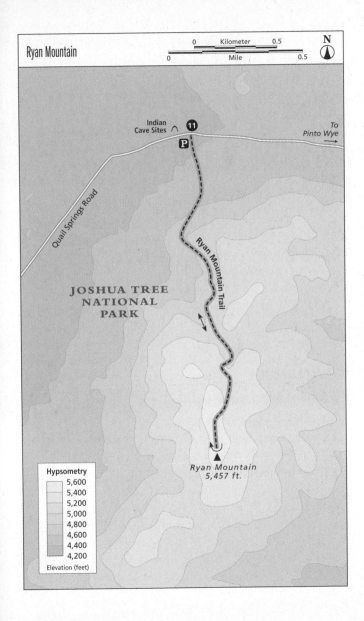

Ryan Mountain

0   Kilometer   0.5

0   Mile   0.5

N

Indian
Cave Sites

11

P

*To
Pinto Wye*

Quail Springs Road

JOSHUA TREE
NATIONAL
PARK

Ryan Mountain Trail

*Ryan Mountain
5,457 ft.*

Hypsometry

5,600
5,400
5,200
5,000
4,800
4,600
4,400
4,200

Elevation (feet)

several hundred million years old. These rocks originated deep within the earth as igneous intrusions in the overlying layers. The jumble of Southern California's tectonic plates created, and continues to create, ruptures that permitted the molten rock to ooze and freeze and await future erosion so it would be exposed.

The trail zigzags only slightly and seeks a relatively gentle slope to the peak's summit, which is at 1.5 miles. A gain of 1,000 feet in 1.5 miles isn't too bad, especially if you take your time, enjoying the view and drinks of water.

If you have spent several days walking nature trails, visiting mine sites, and hiking canyon washes, this 5,457-foot-high peak provides a welcome aerial view of the central portion of the park, including Lost Horse, Queen, and Pleasant Valleys. On your return, don't miss the Indian Cave sites at the western end of the parking area. A sign indicates their location. The fire-stained rock shelters provide a reminder of the centuries of use by human visitors that this silent land has seen.

Miles and Directions

0.0   Begin at the Ryan Mountain trailhead.

0.4   The trail begins a steep climb.

1.5   Reach the summit of Ryan Mountain; retrace your path to the trailhead.

3.0   Arrive back at the trailhead.

12 Desert Queen Mine and Wash

The Desert Queen was the largest and longest operating mine in the park. From the overlook you can view the remains of the mine in the wash below and learn the mine's history.

Distance: 1.2 miles out and back to mine; 4.0 miles out and back down the wash
Approximate hiking time: 1 to 3 hours
Difficulty: Moderate due to slope to mine site and distance for wash walk
Trail surface: Sandy earth, sandy wash with some rocks

Maps: Trails Illustrated Joshua Tree National Park map; USGS Queen Mountain
Trailhead facilities: There is a parking area, a vault toilet, and a backcountry signboard (kiosk) at the end of the dirt Desert Queen Mine Road.

Finding the trailhead: From CA 62 in Twentynine Palms, take Utah Trail south for 4 miles to the park's north entrance. Continue 4.8 miles on Park Boulevard (PR 12) to the Pinto Wye intersection. Stay to the right (southwest) on Park Boulevard (PR 12) and drive 5.1 miles to a right turn on a dirt road immediately opposite the signed Geology Tour Road, which heads south. Turn north on the one-lane, dirt Desert Queen Mine Road and drive 1.4 miles to its end at the Pine City backcountry board and parking area. This unimproved road can be impassable in wet weather or after storms. GPS: N34 1.413' / W116 4.658'

The Hike

This interesting trip covers a variety of mine sites, from the most prosperous in the area (Desert Queen) to those that were obviously not as successful. The Desert Queen was in operation from 1895 to 1961 and was one of the most productive gold mines in the Southern California desert. The debris that is left around the site—and that continues to appear miles down the wash—is also evidence of the environmental repercussions of this industrial use of the desert.

From the parking area, follow the trail eastward to visit the overlook. In addition to getting a bird's-eye view of the mine, you can learn about the Desert Queen's illustrious history from the informative sign. Numerous mine entrances dot the opposite hillside. The magnitude of the Desert Queen operation is revealed by the massive tailings that drip down the mountain into the wash below.

After visiting the overlook, retrace your steps and take the well-traveled trail that leads south off the overlook trail, dropping into the wash. You will pass remnants of a miner's structure en route. The Desert Queen Mine has been fenced off, but caution is still advised while exploring the site. Peeking into these holes in the earth, you have to be impressed with the determination of the early miners with their picks and shovels.

Return to the trailhead by the same route. If you wish to take a longer hike, continue exploring the wash. To the south, which is on your right as you face the mine, is a narrow canyon. Ramble in this direction for 0.5 mile to enjoy a more pristine desert experience. Uphill from the mine, this canyon hasn't received the flow of artifacts that the downstream side has.

Or head on down the wash, to your left (north, then east). The experience of hiking down the wash erases the sight of the damage to the mountainside. The huge boulders that rise above you—and periodically in front of you in the wash, blocking your way at 1.3 and 1.8 miles—are reminders of the forces of nature that are still in operation. The wash's vegetation is profuse and diverse. Mesquite, creosote bush, and smoke trees line the wash, sometimes even blocking your passage. The intermittent power of rushing water has scoured the wash, but these durable plants enjoy this location. You'll also encounter pieces of mining equipment partially buried in the sand. While visiting this area, please keep the park's cultural preservation rules and regulations in mind.

The mining sites farther down the wash represent the other end of the economic spectrum from the Desert Queen. Unlike that operation, the other sites are small. The artifacts found around the miners' dwellings indicate a grim existence for these workers. This was primitive living. The size of the tailings shows that the excavations were not extensive. These mining projects did not last long.

At 2 miles the canyon opens wide, and on your right is a broad flat, slightly elevated above the wash. Here are the remains of John's Camp, once a busy mining community. Roaming around on the flat, you can see traces of humble dwellings left by these hardy souls.

As you walk back up the wash after visiting John's Camp, you can again revel in the beauty of the canyon. Then, turning the last corner, you encounter the mining equipment abandoned in the wash by the Desert Queen. Joshua Tree National Park preserves two very different worlds. We can learn much by being aware of both.

Miles and Directions

0.0   At the trailhead, a cable barricade deters vehicles. The broad trail goes east. The trail to the wash is on your right, going south. Go east to visit the overlook and learn about the mine's history.

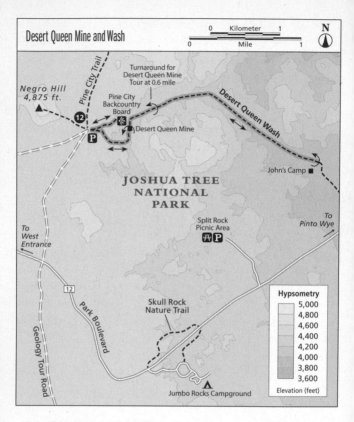

Desert Queen Mine and Wash

Kilometer 1
Mile 1
N

Negro Hill
4,875 ft.

Pine City Trail

Turnaround for
Desert Queen Mine
Tour at 0.6 mile

Pine City
Backcountry
Board

12

P

Desert Queen Mine

Desert Queen Wash

John's Camp

JOSHUA TREE
NATIONAL
PARK

To
West
Entrance

Split Rock
Picnic Area

To
Pinto Wye

12

Park Boulevard

Geology Tour Road

Skull Rock
Nature Trail

Hypsometry
5,000
4,800
4,600
4,400
4,200
4,000
3,800
3,600
Elevation (feet)

Jumbo Rocks Campground

0.1 Reach the overlook. Then retrace your steps back to the trail junction.

0.15 At the trail junction, take the trail leading south to the wash and mine.

0.3 Pass the old stone ruins of a miner's dwelling; the rocky trail winds down to the wash.

0.6 Reach the mining sites. This is the turnaround spot for those not going farther down the wash. Otherwise, continue down the wash toward John's Camp.

1.3 Huge boulders totally block the wash. Take a crude trail on the bank to the right (west).

1.5 The wash widens; an old prospector's site is on a low shelf to the right.

1.8 Another boulder tumble blocks the narrow wash. Follow cairns to the left.

2.0 Bear right to John's Camp site on the low bank. Retrace your path to the trailhead.

4.0 Arrive back at the trailhead.

13 Pine City Site

What a misnomer! This was never a city and the pines are scarce, but it's a lovely green spot to visit. Bighorn sheep are drawn to this desert refuge, especially during summer. The former mining camp is tucked in a picturesque desert ravine with dramatic rock formations. Beyond lies a scenic canyon available for further exploration.

Distance: 3.4 miles out and back, with an optional extension to 4.6 miles out and back
Approximate hiking time: 3 hours
Difficulty: Moderate due to length, but with little change in elevation
Trail surface: Hard earth with some sandy and rocky stretches

Maps: Trails Illustrated Joshua Tree National Park map; USGS Queen Mountain
Trailhead facilities: There is parking, a vault toilet, and a backcountry signboard (kiosk) at the end of the dirt Desert Queen Mine Road.

Finding the trailhead: From CA 62 in Twentynine Palms, take Utah Trail south for 4 miles to the park's north entrance. Continue 4.8 miles on Park Boulevard (PR 12) to the Pinto Wye intersection. Stay right (southwest) on Park Boulevard for 5.1 miles to a dirt road on the right directly opposite the Geology Tour Road. Turn right (north) on the dirt Desert Queen Mine Road and go 1.4 miles to the road's end at the Pine City backcountry board. This unimproved dirt road can be impassable after a desert deluge. GPS: N34 1.413' / W115 4.658'

The Hike

This mellow out-and-back hike leads to the picturesque "day-use-only" former mining camp of Pine City. The optional continuation makes for a more difficult hike past the Pine City site and down into the head of a colorful canyon, with several steep rock pitches.

Except for a few mine shafts grated over for public safety, all that remains of Pine City is the wind rustling through the pines. The one or two cabins that once existed here have been erased by the passage of time. Still, the short, gentle walk to the Pine City site provides ample opportunities for exploration and for savoring its bouldered beauty. The trail maintains an even grade across a high Mojave Desert plateau covered with Joshua trees.

At mile 1.1, an obscure trail leads to the right for 0.2 mile to a picture-perfect pocket of monzoquartz granite ringed with pinyon pines. The main trail to Pine City continues left (north). At 1.6 miles another trail takes off to the right (east), dropping 100 feet in 0.3 mile to the dry Pine Spring. The spring lies just above the narrow notch of a steep, boulder-strewn canyon. This pleasant spot is well suited for a picnic or for just plain relaxing. Bighorn sheep rely on the cool shelter of this place when people are not there.

From the Pine Spring turnoff, continue left (north) another 0.1 mile to the Pine City site, which is immediately east of the trail in a wide, sandy flat next to a huge round boulder sitting atop a rock platform. You could easily spend several hours poking around the myriad side canyons and interesting rock formations that surround the Pine City site. The site contains at least one grated mine shaft and at least one more that is unsecured, so caution should be exercised.

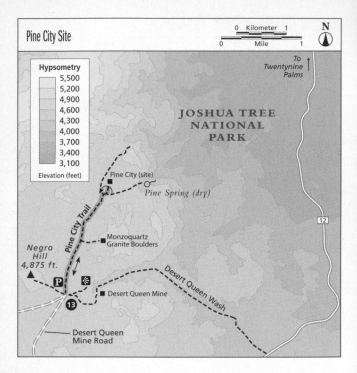

Return the way you came to complete this level 3.4-mile out-and-back hike.

To extend your outing into the upper reaches of Pine City Canyon, stay left (north) on the trail to a point 0.5 mile northeast of the city site, where the trail ends on a ridge next to a small hill, identified as 4,769 feet in elevation on the topo map. Drop into the broad saddle southwest of the hill, and then descend the steep gully to the main Pine City Canyon wash. Continue about 0.1 mile down Pine City Canyon. The route requires some agility, as the boulders frequently block the canyon floor. When time and energy are expended, retrace your path to the trailhead.

Miles and Directions

0.0 Follow the trail north from the Pine City backcountry sign-board and trailhead.

1.1 At the trail junction continue left; the right-hand trail leads to an old mine site with monzoquartz granite boulders.

1.6 Reach a trail intersection. The right-hand trail leads to Pine Spring; continue left to the Pine City site.

1.7 Reach the Pine City site. This is the turnaround for the shorter hike.

3.4 Arrive back at the trailhead.

Option:

2.2 After continuing up the trail from the Pine City site, the trail ends on a ridge above Pine City Canyon.

2.3 A use trail drops to Pine City Canyon. Explore, then retrace your route.

4.6 Arrive back at the trailhead.

14 Skull Rock Nature Trail

These gargantuan bizarre boulders are a magnet for visitors. A Joshua tree forest surrounds the unusual jumbo rock formations. The nature trail's informational signs focus on the geology and ecology of the Mojave Desert.

Distance: 1.7-mile loop
Approximate hiking time: 1.5 hours
Difficulty: Easy
Trail surface: Sandy earth
Maps: Trails Illustrated Joshua Tree National Park map; USGS Malapai Hill
Trailhead facilities: The trail is adjacent to Park Boulevard (PR 12). A vault toilet is available in nearby Jumbo Rocks Campground. The trail can also be accessed from Loop E in the campground.
Other: The park service offers a free ranger program at the Skull Rock Nature Trail. Reservations are not required. Check the schedule online or at a ranger station, as the programs vary seasonally.

Finding the trailhead: From CA 62 in Twentynine Palms, take Utah Trail south for 4 miles to the park's north entrance. Continue south on Park Boulevard (PR 12) for 4.8 miles to the Pinto Wye intersection. Bear right (southwest), still on Park Boulevard, and continue 3.7 miles to the signed Skull Rock Nature Trail trailhead. The parking area is right next to the road. Or you can drive into the Jumbo Rocks Campground and begin the trail at the end of Loop E. GPS: N33 59.871' / W 116 3.597'

The Hike

Park Boulevard divides this loop trail. The northern half of the loop begins at the Skull Rock sign on the highway and starts out northward; at 0.7 mile it ends at the Jumbo Rocks

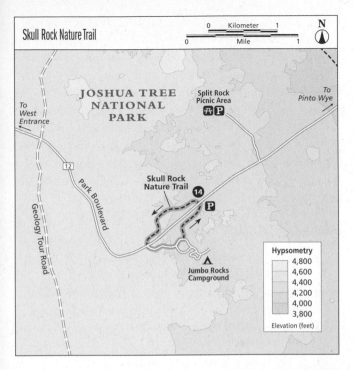

Campground entrance. To pick up the other half of the trail from there, it is necessary to walk 0.5 mile down through the campground to the end of Loop E.

The northern half of the loop is more rustic. The route meanders along parallel to the road, winding between rock formations and through shallow gullies. There are several interpretive signs. The trail is marked with rocks and can always be discerned in the sandy soil. The eroded boulders are spectacular sights. Basic geology, plant identification, and desert survival tips are intermixed in the interpretive signs.

Cross the road at the Jumbo Rocks Campground at 0.7 mile, then follow the road 0.5 mile through the campground to the southern section of the trail, which begins at a sign on Loop E. On the southern half of the loop, the interpretive signs are updated, more plentiful, and more instructive. They focus on desert diversity and the interconnectedness of the plants and animals that make this region their home. The famous, aptly named, and much-photographed Skull Rock sits at the end of the southern loop, immediately adjacent to the road. Skull Rock itself is quite forbidding, and the other formations on the route are equally fascinating and thought-provoking. This is an excellent family outing for photography and for leisurely exploration.

Miles and Directions

0.0 Begin at the Skull Rock Nature Trail trailhead on Park Boulevard (PR 12). Cross the road to pick up the trail.

0.7 Cross the road to the Jumbo Rocks Campground. Walk to Loop E.

1.2 Reach the end of campground Loop E; resume the nature trail.

1.7 Complete the loop back at the trailhead.

15 Arch Rock Nature Trail

A short nature trail winds around fascinating White Tank granite formations and features appropriate geology lessons. This is a good rock scramble for agile kids, and a good romp for the restless family staying at the White Tank Campground. Please note: The popularity of this trail has made parking an occasionally difficult task.

Distance: 0.3-mile loop
Approximate hiking time: 30 minutes
Difficulty: Easy
Trail surface: Sandy earth

Maps: Trails Illustrated Joshua Tree National Park map; USGS Malapai Hill
Trailhead facilities: The signed trailhead is adjacent to the White Tank Campground, where a vault toilet is available.

Finding the trailhead: From CA 62 in Twentynine Palms, take Utah Trail south for 4 miles to the north entrance of the park. Continue south on Park Boulevard (PR 12) for 4.8 miles to the Pinto Wye intersection. Turn left (south) at the wye intersection onto Pinto Basin Road (PR 11) and go 2.8 miles to White Tank Campground, which is on your left (east). Turn in to the campground and follow the nature trail sign to the trailhead, which is on the left immediately after the campground information board. GPS: N33 59.162' / W116 1.018'

The Hike

This nature trail focuses on the unique geology of the fascinating rock formations that abound in this area of the park. The informational signs present a sophisticated series of geology lessons, far beyond the simplistic rock identification

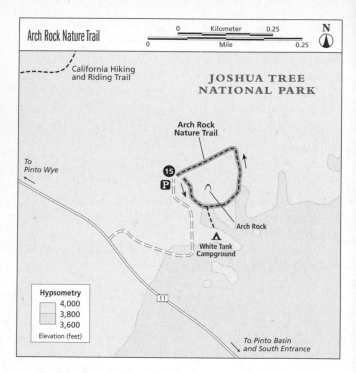

usually found on such trails. The trail itself is an adventure in geology as it winds through fantastic boulders to the famed Arch Rock at 0.1 mile.

The trip through the geology lesson covers igneous rock formation, the origins of White Tank granite, erosion, selective erosion, dikes, faults, and how natural arches are formed. The remainder of your visit in the park will be greatly enhanced by this knowledge.

For a slightly longer hike, visit White Tank. At the Arch Rock exhibit on the nature trail, walk in front of Arch Rock and continue about 100 yards to the southeast, where you will arrive at an old sanded-in cattle tank. These artifacts of ranching days in Joshua Tree have become good habitat for birds and other desert creatures. Shrubs enjoy the residual subterranean moisture captured by the tanks, providing cover for wildlife.

Miles and Directions

0.0 Begin at the Arch Rock Nature Trail trailhead. Go right on the loop trail.

0.1 Reach Arch Rock. Take a side trip to White Tank if desired.

0.3 Arrive back at the trailhead.

Southern Zone

16 Silver Bell Mine

Defunct mines have a magical attraction for many park visitors. It's not only that eerie hole in the ground but also the elaborate engineering necessary for the operation. Here at the Silver Bell, the two tipples remain on the hillside above the mine, perfectly preserved in the dry desert air. The mine is called the Golden Bell on the topo map.

Distance: 1.4 miles out and back
Approximate hiking time: 1 to 2 hours
Difficulty: Moderately strenuous due to elevation gain (250 feet) and rocky path

Trail surface: Rocky desert and eroded mining road
Maps: Trails Illustrated Joshua Tree National Park map; USGS Fried Liver Wash
Trailhead facilities: There is parking along Pinto Basin Road.

Finding the trailhead: From CA 62 in Twentynine Palms, take Utah Trail south for 4 miles to the park's north entrance. Continue for 4.8 miles south on Park Boulevard (PR 12) to the Pinto Wye intersection. Turn left (south) onto Pinto Basin Road (PR 11). The turnout for the Silver Bell site is on the right (south), just south of milepost 8, 4.3 miles south of the wye intersection. GPS: N33 55.937' / W115 57.397'

The Hike

This outing is more adventuresome than a nature trail, but you are seldom out of sight of the tipples or the road on the entire route. The trailhead sign explains the history of the Silver Bell, which produced gold, lead, and copper from the 1930s to the 1950s. From this vantage point you can see your path, the old mine road sloping up the hillside to the tipples. Head off across the desert in this direction. A path is intermittently visible, but since it's erased periodically by erosive floods, it's not always clear.

At the foot of the hillside you will meet the mining road. This leads up to the mine opening. You can see the posts that restrict access to the gaping hole on the hillside above you. Adjacent to the adit are the rocky remains of a prospector dwelling. Miners didn't like to be far from their mines to protect them from interlopers. And comfort was not on the list of priorities. Gazing out on the valley floor below, you can spot other mining remains scattered about.

Drop back down to the mining road and continue your hike up the road to the tipples. Go around the metal posts that the park installed to deter vehicles, and continue up to the top. The view from here is inspiring. From the mouth of Wilson Canyon, the vast Pinto Basin stretches to the hazy mountain ranges in the distance.

The construction of these large industrial bins—the tipples—so far from a lumberyard is extraordinary. These prospectors were skillful engineers. They knew what they were doing, and their lives depended on their skills.

As always, be careful when exploring the site, and keep an eye on children and any foolish adults in your party. Old mines are hazardous.

Retrace your steps to the trailhead.

Miles and Directions

0.0 From the trailhead, head toward the sloping mining road south of the highway.

0.3 Reach the foot of the mining road and the nearby trail to the mine adit.

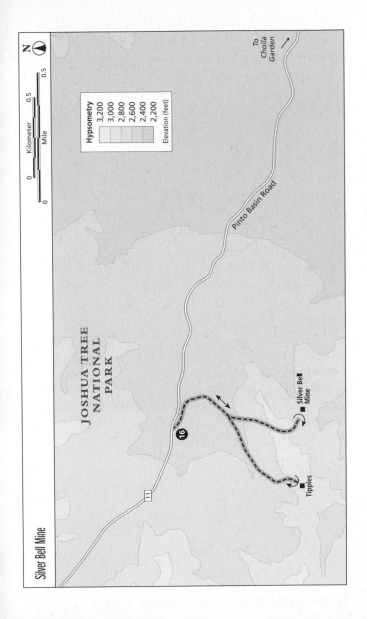

Silver Bell Mine

JOSHUA TREE
NATIONAL
PARK

Pinto Basin Road

Silver Bell
Mine

Tipples

To
Cholla
Garden

N

Hypsometry
3,200
3,000
2,800
2,600
2,400
2,200
Elevation (feet)

Kilometer
0   0.5
Mile
0   0.5

11

16

0.4 Arrive at the mine adit. Return to the mining road. Continue uphill on the road.

0.7 Arrive at the tipples. Retrace your path to the trailhead.

1.4 Arrive back at the trailhead.

17 Cholla Cactus Garden Nature Trail

An unusually dense stand of cholla cactus rises in a cluster above the vast Pinto Basin. The plants are as captivating as the views of the desert and the mountain ranges that surround the trail.

Distance: 0.25-mile loop
Approximate hiking time: 30 minutes
Difficulty: Easy
Trail surface: Level sandy earth

Maps: Trails Illustrated Joshua Tree National Park map; USGS Fried Liver Wash
Trailhead facilities: There is a signed parking area next to the paved highway.

Finding the trailhead: From CA 62 in Twentynine Palms, take Utah Trail south for 4 miles to the park's north entrance. Continue for 4.8 miles south on Park Boulevard (PR 12) to the Pinto Wye intersection. Turn left (south) onto Pinto Basin Road (PR 11). The Cholla Cactus Garden parking area is on the right (south) near milepost 10, 6.3 miles south of the wye intersection. GPS: N33 55.938' / W115 55.754'

The Hike

This massive array of cholla cacti, common in the Colorado (Sonoran) Desert, is impressive even when it is not in bloom. There is intense bee activity at the garden (and in many other locations throughout the park). Those with sensitivity to, or phobias of, bees should avoid visiting here during the pollination season. For others, the flowering of the cholla is an exuberant explosion of color.

Cholla Cactus Garden Nature Trail

0 ⸻ Kilometer ⸻ 0.25

0 ⸻ Mile ⸻ 0.25

N

JOSHUA TREE
NATIONAL
PARK

To
Pinto Wye

11

17 P

Pinto Basin Road

Cholla Cactus
Garden Nature
Trail

To
South Entrance

Hypsometry

2,400
2,200
2,000
Elevation (feet)

This is a self-guided trail with pamphlets available at the entrance. The information will broaden your perception of life in the desert. But even without a pamphlet for interpretation, the high density of Bigelow cholla, known as "teddy bear cactus," is impressive. Cholla cactus has another name, not as cuddly as the teddy bear one—"jumping cactus." The balls of spines easily detach from the plant if you touch it, as if they're jumping at you. The sea of cholla extends well beyond the garden's fenced area, although this particular side slope is unique in the park.

Panoramic views of the surrounding Hexie Mountains, the Pinto Range, and the vast Pinto Basin combine to make the Cholla Cactus Garden a spectacular spot on the edge of this southern desert region.

Miles and Directions

0.0 The path begins at the fence. Head right (counterclockwise) around the loop.

0.25 Complete the loop at the trailhead.

18 Mastodon Peak

This loop hike begins near a lush desert spring, climbs to a mill site, and continues on to the remnants of a historic mine. The lumpy monzogranite mound on which the mine is located reminded early visitors of a prehistoric creature. A side trip to the top of the peak provides a panoramic view of the area.

Distance: 2.6-mile loop
Approximate hiking time: 2 to 3 hours
Difficulty: Moderately strenuous due to the 440-foot elevation gain and some boulders
Trail surface: Sandy earth with some rocks and boulders
Maps: Trails Illustrated Joshua Tree National Park map; USGS Cottonwood Spring

Trailhead facilities: The paved parking area is near the Cottonwood Campground and has a vault toilet.
Other: The park service has a 2.5-hour ranger program on the Mastodon Peak Trail. It's free, and reservations are not required. Check the park website or at the Cottonwood Ranger Station for the schedule.

Finding the trailhead: From CA 62 in Twentynine Palms, take Utah Trail south for 4 miles to the park's north entrance. Continue 4.8 miles on Park Boulevard (PR 12) to the Pinto Wye intersection. Turn left (south) onto Pinto Basin Road (PR 11) and go south for 32 miles to the Cottonwood Visitor Center. Turn left (east) and go 1.5 miles to the end of the road at the Cottonwood Spring oasis.

From the south, take the Cottonwood Canyon exit from I-10, which is 24 miles east of Indio. Go north for 8 miles to the Cottonwood Visitor Center. Turn right (east) and go 1.5 miles to the end of the road at the Cottonwood Spring parking lot. GPS: N33 44.21400' / W115 48.64380'

The Hike

A moderate 2.6-mile loop hike leads from the Cottonwood Spring oasis to nearby Winona Mill, Mastodon Mine, and Mastodon Peak. The peak requires some scrambling, but it provides impressive views of the southern section of the park, the Eagle Mountains, and the Salton Sea.

To begin the hike, walk west from the parking lot, back up the road, for 0.1 mile to the beginning of the Cottonwood Spring Nature Trail, which is on your right. Walk up the nature trail for 0.3 mile to the junction with the Mastodon Peak Trail. From the Cottonwood Campground, the trail begins 0.5 mile from campsite 13A on Loop A, via the nature trail segment that begins at the campground and meets at the same junction.

Whether you begin at the campground or the oasis, both approaches to the Mastodon trail include the nature trail, whose theme is Native American subsistence in the Sonoran Desert. The view of the old gold mill and the mine is in direct contrast with the Native Americans' use of the riches of the desert; the latter left no ruins or scars on the environment.

Signposts and a rock-lined path clearly mark the Mastodon Peak Trail. The lower section of the hike is up a sandy wash to the Winona Mill site, 0.2 mile from the trail junction. Building foundations and scattered relics are all that remain of the mill that refined gold from the Mastodon Mine in the 1920s. The Hulsey family, which owned the mill and mine, established the plant specimens at the adjacent Cottonwood Spring.

The trail winds up the hill above the mill to the Mastodon Mine, which was operated by George Hulsey between

1919 and 1932, when it was abandoned. Carefully thread your way up by the sign above the mine, which is at 1 mile. The trail gives you no choice but to pick a path through the mine ruins to the trail post and arrow pointing east on the other side of the mine site. A major freeway-style sign indicates your options and the various distances to the spring, the oasis, and the peak from this point.

The 0.1-mile climb to the peak is on an unsigned trail, although the well-used path is easy to discern and cairns mark critical spots. This portion of the hike is for more vigorous travelers; those for whom it is sufficient to survey Mastodon Peak from below may continue on the trail looping around to the right. The use trail to the peak goes to the right of a boulder pile, across a slab of granite, and winds around the northeast side of the peak to the summit, on the opposite side from the mine site. Minor boulder scrambling is necessary, but the view is well worth the effort.

After leaving the peak, the trail resumes a zigzag, rocky path down the ridge and through the canyon, well signed with arrows. On this portion of the trail you can clearly see the elephant likeness in the peak behind you. The intersection with the Lost Palms Oasis Trail is about 0.5 mile beyond the peak, at 1.6 miles. Turn right (northwest) for the 1-mile walk down the winding trail to Cottonwood Spring and the ramp to the parking lot.

Miles and Directions

0.0 To begin, take the Cottonwood Spring Nature Trail from the parking lot.

0.3 Reach the Mastodon Peak Trail junction and turn right.

0.5 Pass the Winona Mill ruins and Cotton Spring.

1.0 Arrive at Mastodon Mine. The trail continues above the mine.

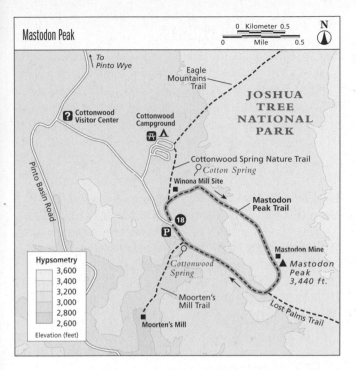

0   Kilometer   0.5

0   Mile   0.5

N

To
Pinto Wye

Eagle
Mountains
Trail

JOSHUA
TREE
NATIONAL
PARK

Cottonwood
Visitor Center

Cottonwood
Campground

Cottonwood Spring Nature Trail
Cotton Spring

Winona Mill Site

Mastodon
Peak Trail

Pinto Basin Road

18
P

Mastodon Mine

Mastodon
Peak
3,440 ft.

Hypsometry

3,600
3,400
3,200
3,000
2,800
2,600

Elevation (feet)

Cottonwood
Spring

Moorten's
Mill Trail

Moorten's Mill

Lost Palms Trail

1.1 At the trail junction, go left to the peak (0.1-mile round-trip).

1.6 Reach the Lost Palms Oasis Trail junction. Turn right to return to the parking area.

2.6 Arrive at the Cottonwood Spring trailhead. Continue up the ramp to the parking area.

19 Lost Palms Oasis

Tucked away in a narrow canyon, this hidden oasis features the largest grove of California fan palms in the park. Unlike Fortynine Palms Oasis on the northern edge of Joshua Tree National Park, this lush spot is protected from vandalism by its seclusion. The contrast with the long dry trail makes the oasis especially enjoyable. It is an excellent spot for birding.

Distance: 7.6 miles out and back, with a 9.6-mile extended hike option to Victory Palms
Approximate hiking time: 4 to 5 hours
Difficulty: Moderately strenuous due to length and rolling hills
Trail surface: Sandy earth with sandy washes

Maps: Trails Illustrated Joshua Tree National Park map; USGS Cottonwood Spring
Trailhead facilities: There is a signed parking area at the end of the paved access road. A vault toilet is at the nearby Cottonwood Campground, or you can find a real one at the Cottonwood Visitor Center.

Finding the trailhead: From CA 62 in Twentynine Palms, on the north side of the park, take Utah Trail south for 4 miles to the park's north entrance. Continue south on Park Boulevard (PR 12) for 4.8 miles to the Pinto Wye intersection. Turn left (south) onto Pinto Basin Road (PR 11) and go 32 miles to the Cottonwood Visitor Center. Turn left (east) and go 1.5 miles to the Cottonwood Spring parking area.

From the south, take the Cottonwood Canyon exit from I-10, 24 miles east of Indio. Go north for 8 miles on Cottonwood Spring Road to the Cottonwood Visitor Center. Turn right (east) and go 1.5 miles to the Cottonwood Spring parking area. GPS: N33 44.214' / W115 48.643'

The Hike

From the parking area above Cottonwood Spring, follow the paved sidewalk down to the spring and take the marked trail on your left. This is a dry, high hike, with no protection from sun and wind. It is a heavily signed route with mileage posts, along with arrows at every bend and every wash crossing.

The first mile of the Lost Palms hike corresponds with the Mastodon Peak Trail. You will reach that signed junction on a ridge and continue straight (southeast) on the oasis trail.

The trail follows the up-and-down topography of the ridge-and-wash terrain. At each ridge you'll hope to spot the oasis ahead, particularly if it is a hot and sunny day. Not until the final overlook will such hopes be realized. After crossing numerous ridges, descending rocky paths to narrow canyons, and winding up to more ridges, it is a welcome sight!

This is the largest group of California fan palms in Joshua Tree National Park, and they are majestic. This marvelous grove extends about 0.5 mile down the valley. The oasis is within a day-use-only area to protect bighorn sheep's access to water. You may be lucky enough to spot one of the elusive animals on the rocky slopes above or near the oasis, particularly during hot periods, when they are most in need of water. A rocky path leads 0.4 mile from the overlook, which is at 3.4 miles, to the oasis. Large boulders, pools of water, intermittent streams, willow thickets, and sandy beaches make this a delightful spot to pause. Retrace your steps to the parking area.

Option: The more energetic hiker may wish to continue down the canyon through the willows and around the pools, following an intermittent rusty pipe that was used to channel water to a mining site far to the south. The trail becomes

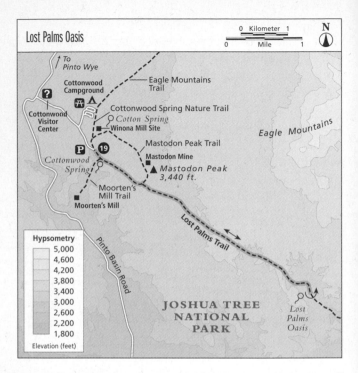

more challenging, with larger boulders to contend with along the way. The Victory Palms are located about 1 mile below the upper end of the Lost Palms Oasis. When your desire for rock scrambling is satisfied, it is time to return to the oasis and retrace your steps to Cottonwood Spring.

Miles and Directions

- **0.0** The trail begins above the oasis at Cottonwood Spring; take the trail to the left at the spring.
- **1.0** The Mastodon Peak Trail goes to the left. Continue straight (southeast) to the oasis.
- **2.1** The trail descends to a wash.

3.0 Descend down a narrow crumbly ridge to a narrow wash.

3.4 Reach the Lost Palms Oasis overlook; this is a good turn-around point for a shorter hike.

3.8 Arrive at the floor of the oasis.

7.6 Arrive back at the trailhead.

Option:

4.8 Continue from the oasis to Victory Palms. Retrace your steps to the trailhead.

9.6 Arrive back at the trailhead.

20 Cottonwood Spring Nature Trail/ Moorten's Mill Site

The Cottonwood Spring Nature Trail not only provides iden-
tifications of desert plants but also describes their uses by Native
Americans. A stroll farther down from Cottonwood Spring
allows you to see another use of the desert at Moorten's Mill.

Distance: 1.6 miles out and
back for the nature trail; 1.0 mile
out and back for the mill
Approximate hiking time: 1 to
2 hours
Difficulty: Easy
Trail surface: Sandy earth, sandy
wash, and a short rocky stretch
of mine road
Maps: Trails Illustrated Joshua
Tree National Park map; USGS
Cottonwood Spring

Trailhead facilities: The parking
area is adjacent to the Cottonwood Campground.
Other: The park service has an
informative ranger program at
Cottonwood Spring. It's free, and
reservations are not necessary.
Check the park website or at the
nearby Cottonwood Ranger Station for the schedule.

Finding the trailhead: From CA 62 in Twentynine Palms, on the
north side of the park, take Utah Trail south for 4 miles to the park's
north entrance. Continue for 4.8 miles on Park Boulevard (PR 12) to
the Pinto Wye intersection. Turn left (south) onto Pinto Basin Road
(PR 11) and go south for 32 miles to the Cottonwood Visitor Center.
Turn left (east) and follow the access road 1.5 miles to the oasis and
trailhead.

From the south, take the Cottonwood Canyon exit from I-10, which is 24
miles east of Indio. Go north for 8 miles to the Cottonwood Visitor Center,
then right (east) for 1.5 miles to the Cottonwood Spring oasis parking lot.

The nature trail also has entrances at the eastern ends of Loops A and B in the campground, but if you're not camping, it is not possible to park at the campground. GPS: N33 44.214' / W115 48.643'

The Hike

The nature trail begins 0.1 mile back up the paved road from the parking area. This broad clear trail leads up a wash from the road near the spring, eventually winding up to a low ridge leading to the campground. This is one of the most informative nature trails in the park. The signs are legible, accurately placed, and highly educational.

The information on this nature trail identifies plants native to the Sonoran Desert. The signs focus on the Cahuilla Indians' use of plants for food, medicine, and household goods. A Cahuilla elder provided the information. The detailed explanations of the processes used by the original inhabitants create genuine admiration for their sophistication. Several of the plants originally utilized by the Native Americans, such as the creosote bush and jojoba, are now grown and marketed commercially.

After reaching the end of the nature trail near the campground, retrace your steps to the parking lot, reviewing the information you have learned. Then visit Cottonwood Spring, which is located down the ramp at the foot of the parking area. Cottonwood Spring is a lovely patch of greenery in an otherwise arid landscape. Miners planted the cottonwoods and fan palms around the turn of the twentieth century to make the spring conform to their concept of an oasis. The sight, as well as the sound, of greenery is satisfying, and obviously the birds enjoy the location.

To visit the Moorten's Mill site, hike down from the spring, enjoying the display of a Sonoran Desert wash plant community. Mesquite and smoke trees are dominant. Posts mark this segment of the hike, since footprints are washed away by intermittent rains. After winter rains the sandy surface below the spring is damp, causing great joy for wildlife.

At 0.25 mile, boulders block the wash in a narrow stretch called Little Chilcoot Pass. To the right, miners constructed a section of road in the 1880s. Their determination to use this route for their vehicles is noteworthy. The stone-and-earth ramp they built is massive. Yet even with it in place, the trek up or down the wash must have been arduous with a heavily loaded wagon. After you descend on the lumpy road, look back at the obstacle that blocked the miners—a 30-foot pour-off—and you can't help but be awed by their determination to get around it.

Continue on down the sandy wash for another 0.25 mile. A solitary post with an arrow is in the middle of the wash here. On your right, where the canyon widens, is the mill site. Seeing this site will cure any thoughts of romanticizing the prospector's life in these parts. While the wash is lovely for its solitude and silence, living here must have been grim. "Cactus" Slim Moorten (or Morten) operated a stamp mill here for less than ten years. Only rusty equipment and rusting car parts remain.

The hike back up the wash and over Little Chilcoot Pass brings you back to the oasis, which looks even greener after a sojourn in drier country.

Miles and Directions

Cottonwood Spring Nature Trail

0.0 Begin at the Cottonwood Spring trailhead. Walk back up the road to the trail.

0.1 Turn right (north) on the nature trail.

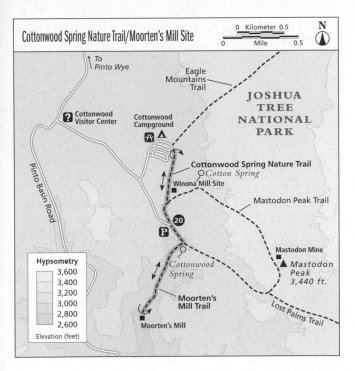

Cottonwood Spring Nature Trail/Moorten's Mill Site

0   Kilometer   0.5

0   Mile   0.5

N

To
Pinto Wye

Eagle
Mountains
Trail

**JOSHUA
TREE
NATIONAL
PARK**

Cottonwood
Visitor Center

Cottonwood
Campground

Cottonwood Spring Nature Trail

Cotton Spring

Winona Mill Site

Mastodon Peak Trail

Pinto Basin Road

20

P

Mastodon Mine

Cottonwood
Spring

▲ Mastodon
Peak
3,440 ft.

Hypsometry

3,600
3,400
3,200
3,000
2,800
2,600

Elevation (feet)

**Moorten's
Mill Trail**

Moorten's Mill

Lost Palms Trail

0.3 At the Mastodon Peak Trail junction, the trail continues north to the campground.

0.8 Arrive at the campground. Retrace your path to the spring.

1.6 Having visited the spring, arrive back at the trailhead.

Moorten's Mill Hike

0.0 From the parking lot, take the ramp down to the oasis.

0.1 Stay in the wash and continue south.

0.25 Reach Little Chilcoot Pass. The trail continues on your right.

0.5 Arrive at the Moorten's Mill site, with a trail post in the center of the wash. Retrace your path to the trailhead.

1.0 Arrive back at the trailhead.

About the Authors

Polly and Bill Cunningham are lifelong hikers and wilderness advocates. They have collaborated on several FalconGuides, including *Wild Utah*, *Hiking New Mexico's Gila Wilderness*, *Hiking New Mexico's Aldo Leopold Wilderness*, *Best Easy Day Hikes Joshua Tree*, *Hiking California's Desert Parks*, *Hiking Mojave National Preserve*, *Hiking Joshua Tree National Park*, *Hiking Death Valley National Park*, and *Hiking Anza-Borrego Desert National Park*.

Bruce Grubbs is an avid camper, backpacker, hiker, mountain biker, and cross-country skier who has been exploring the American desert for over thirty years. A professional outdoor writer and photographer, he has written many previous FalconGuides, including *Hiking Arizona*. He lives in Flagstaff, Arizona.